WORLD OF
MAMMALS

FOXES

By Sophie Lockwood

Content Adviser: Barbara E. Brown, Scientific Associate, Mammal Division, Field Museum of Chicago

THE CHILD'S WORLD®, MANKATO, MINNESOTA

Foxes

Published in the United States of America by The Child's World®
1980 Lookout Drive • Mankato, MN 56003-1705
800-599-READ • www.childsworld.com

Acknowledgements:

The Child's World®: Mary Berendes, Publishing Director

The Creative Spark: Mary Francis, Project Director; Wendy Mead, Editor; Deborah Goodsite, Photo Researcher

The Design Lab: Kathleen Petelinsek, Designer and Production Artist

Photos:

Cover: Natalia Bratslavsky/iStockphoto.com; frontispiece and page 4: David Meharey/iStockphoto.com; half title: Karel Broz/Photoka/Dreamstime.com.

Interior: Alamy: 9 (tbkmedia.de), 5 top right and 14 (Arco Images), 16, 26 (blickwinkel), 5 bottom left and 36–37 (Bruce Coleman Inc.); Animals Animals—Earth Scenes: 5 bottom right and 24 (E. Bartov/OSF); AP Photo: 32 (Paul Ellis), 35 (Kevork Djansezian); Jupiterimages: 5 top left and 10 (Daniel Cox/Oxford Scientific), 23 (Stan Osolinski/Oxford Scientific), 28 (Oxford Scientific); Minden Pictures: 5 center left and 19 (Andrew Cooper/npl), 20–21 (Anup Shah/npl); Photo Researchers, Inc.: 30 (Helen Williams); Visuals Unlimited: 12 (Tom J. Ulrich).

Library of Congress Cataloging-in-Publication Data

Lockwood, Sophie.
  Foxes / by Sophie Lockwood.
    p. cm. — (The world of mammals)
  Includes index.
  ISBN 978-1-59296-932-6 (library bound : alk. paper)
  1. Foxes--Juvenile literature. I. Title. II. Series.
  QL737.C22L63 2008
  599.775—dc22   2007021943

TABLE OF CONTENTS

Chapter One

Thriving in the Arctic

On the frozen tundra of Canada, a white fox follows a polar bear from a distance. The fox huddles low on the ice. He watches and waits. The polar bear comes to a **polynya,** an opening in the ice pack. The bear, too, settles down to wait. The bear knows that seals use the polynya to rise to the surface and breathe.

The bear is a skilled hunter. When a ringed seal breaks the water's surface, the bear grasps it. The polar bear eats the seal's blubber and leaves the meat behind. The Arctic fox gets a free meal after the polar bear leaves. This is one way that Arctic foxes (*Vulpes lagopus*) survive in a climate where few other mammals live through the winter.

An Arctic fox can survive in temperatures as low as −50°C (−58°F). The fox's fur has a thick inner coat that prevents the animal from losing body heat. Hair coats its feet to protect the pads from the cold. The muzzle and ears are short, which is another way the Arctic fox keeps its body heat from escaping.

Did You Know?
Sometimes Arctic foxes use dens that may be three hundred years old. These dens have many tunnels and up to one hundred entrances. Most times, however, they build their own dens on the tundra with four to twelve entrances.

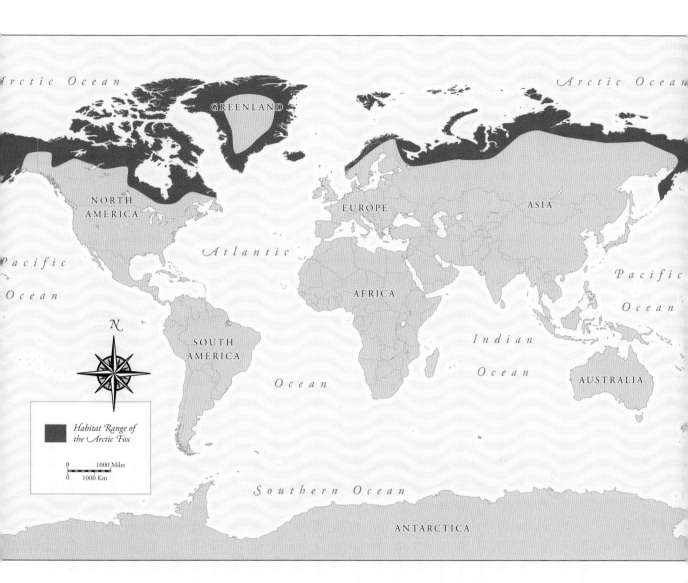

The Arctic fox's den, called an earth, is located above the frozen **permafrost.** Foxes choose rock piles or low, earthen mounds for denning. Good denning sites are few, so the foxes use their dens repeatedly.

This map shows the habitat range for the Arctic fox.

Arctic foxes can produce young before they reach one year old. A dog fox (male) and a vixen (female) mate in April or May. By late spring, Arctic foxes have shed their thick white fur, revealing a brownish-gray summer coat.

After a pregnancy of about fifty days, the vixen gives birth to nine pups. Arctic foxes have the largest litters of any mammals, ranging from three to eleven pups, with a maximum litter size of nineteen. The newborns weigh about 57 grams (2 ounces). The pups begin to peek outside the den at about three to four weeks old. By five weeks, the vixen begins weaning the pups from nursing, and then the really hard work begins.

This year is a remarkably good year for lemmings. These black and tan rodents make up the bulk of the Arctic fox's diet. When the pups begin to eat solid food, the dog and vixen chew the meat and **regurgitate** it for the pups.

The growing pups are always hungry. The parents hunt from late afternoon to midmorning the next day. Each parent hunts eight to ten times per night, catching on average six lemmings each hunt. By the time the pups are fully grown and ready to be on their own, at about four or five months, the parent foxes will have supplied 3,500 to 4,000 lemmings. Parenting a litter of Arctic fox pups is exhausting business.

Arctic foxes live on the tundra of Alaska, Canada, Greenland, Iceland, Scandinavia, and Russia. In years when lemmings

A mother Artic fox rests with her pups.

Did You Know?
Arctic foxes are opportunistic feeders—they eat anything, alive or dead, that opportunity presents. This includes rodents, seaweed, berries, birds and eggs, fish, insects, and insect larvae. They also store food for later feedings.

are plentiful—three hundred or four hundred to an acre of land—Arctic foxes thrive. Unfortunately for foxes, lemmings have a four-year cycle during which the population increases, then plunges. When Arctic foxes face a lemming crash, they **migrate** to find food. Foxes may migrate as much as 1,000 kilometers (620 miles) during one season. Canadian Arctic foxes may move to Greenland, traveling over pack ice. Some foxes survive. Others die of starvation. The life of an Arctic fox is a difficult one.

Did You Know?
Arctic foxes move about their homeland more than any other land-based mammal except for humans.

An Arctic fox roams on the ice pack in Canada.

Chapter Two

Muzzle to Brush

A red fox slips along the edge of a meadow. Its sharp eyes pick up the movement of a field mouse among the wildflowers. The fox holds perfectly still, and then it pounces! Pouncing is a technique that foxes work hard to perfect. It is the best way to catch mice, voles, rabbits, and birds that nest, feed, and live on the ground. It is also a technique commonly used by cats. Foxes have catlike hunting skills, catlike teeth, and catlike claws, and are about the size of a cat. Yet foxes are related to dogs, wolves, coyotes, jackals, dholes, and African wild dogs.

Not all foxes are true foxes. Those that scientists list as true foxes belong to the **genus** *Vulpes*. The number of foxes in that grouping changes as scientists learn more about fox and foxlike species. Today, scientists list twelve species of *Vulpes*. Only a few years

Did You Know?
Male foxes are called dogs, tods, or reynards. Females are called vixens. Young may be called whelps, pups, kits, or cubs. A group of foxes is called a skulk.

Like other foxes, red foxes have pointed ears, thick fur, and a long tail.

ago, *Vulpes* included just ten species. Arctic, crab-eating, bat-eared, and gray foxes are not *Vulpes* foxes, but they are called foxes nonetheless.

Foxes have long bodies that they keep low to the ground. Their legs are short compared to most members of the family Canidae. A fox's muzzle is distinctive—long, narrow, and pointed. The ears are also pointed and fairly large compared to the body. Foxes need large ears because, being night hunters, they depend heavily on their hearing.

The outstanding feature on every species of fox is the tail. Called brushes or sweeps, fox tails can range from 40 to 100 percent of the animals' body length. A fox's tail provides balance when the fox leaps. It also keeps the fox warm. Foxes curl up on cold nights and cover their muzzles with their fluffy, warm tails. When danger strikes, the white-tipped tail rises into the air like a flag.

Fox fur ranges from red to dark brown on the most common species, the red fox. Arctic foxes have white to bluish-gray fur during the winter. Desert fox species are generally buff or tan colored. Fox fur has two layers, a dense undercoat and a longer-haired overcoat. The undercoat keeps foxes warm in bitter cold and protects desert fox species from the sun's heat.

FOX CHATTER

While wolves and coyotes howl, foxes **gekker.** Gekkering is a means of fox communication. The gekkering noise sounds like the fox is clearing its throat. Foxes gekker when they are courting and when pups play. Fox voices range five full octaves, and each fox has its own distinctive voice. Foxes chatter quietly when they are close together in a den. Over distances, they use louder sounds to communicate. A loud bark might announce danger, and the warning needs to be heard by all foxes in the area. Another sound made by foxes is the vixen's wail. This long, eerie cry is named for the females, but males also wail on occasion.

Two red fox pups "talk" to each other.

QUICK, SLY, AND ALERT

Foxes have a reputation for being sly or clever. It may be that they are lucky or, that they rely on advance planning. When humans hunt foxes, they are amazed by how quickly a fox finds a den to hide in. This should be no surprise, since foxes dig long tunnels in their dens and equip the tunnels with dozens of exits.

Foxes rely on excellent senses of sight, hearing, and smell when finding prey or getting themselves out of trouble. Swift foxes see the twitch of individual blades of grass as a mouse moves past, looking for food. Bat-eared foxes (*Otocyon megalotis*), which are not "true" foxes, have huge ears—ranging in size from 114 to 135 millimeters (4.5 to 5.3 inches) long—that they use to hear beetle larvae eating their way through dung balls. A red fox smells a nest of young rabbits hidden behind tall grasses.

Acute senses are helpful in finding food, and foxes are not picky eaters. They will eat any type of meat, insect, or fish. They also feed on carrion, which they find by scent. Like bears, foxes are considered omnivores—they eat both meat and plants. Foxes particularly enjoy berries, melons, tomatoes, bananas, and seaweed. When food is plentiful, foxes **cache** their extra

Did You Know?
Foxes have been known to charm their prey. They dance about, leaping, somersaulting, and rolling around. A bird, vole, or rabbit becomes curious and stops to watch—and the fox pounces on its dinner.

food. A cache of rabbits will rot, but the fox does not mind eating rotting flesh. Protein is protein, and a fox's digestive tract allows for eating both the rotting flesh and the insects crawling on it. Eating a wide variety of foods and storing food for later when it is plentiful are both part of the fox's survival plan.

A Cape fox carries its prey—a striped mouse.

Chapter Three

Highly Adaptable Species

A fox chows down on a delectable feast—half a piece of fried fish and a dozen discarded French fries. This vixen is one of more than ten thousand foxes that live within the city limits of London, England. Yes, this is an urban fox, and the vixen feeds on rats, mice, and human garbage. Foxes are one of the few wild species that actually thrive when in contact with humans.

Foxes can adapt to just about any environment. Arctic foxes live above the Arctic Circle. Fennec, Ruppell's, and **pallid** foxes dwell in the Sahara. Tibetan foxes live high on the Tibetan Plateau of Asia, while kit foxes roam dry Southern California valleys.

In most areas, foxes keep to a nighttime, or **nocturnal,** schedule. Their normal prey feeds at night, so the foxes do, too. Night hunting suits foxes living in cities

Did You Know?
London foxes have invaded the Houses of Parliament (England's main government building) and Buckingham Palace (the London home of Queen Elizabeth).

because fewer people are around to disturb them. If a fox feels secure in its environment, it may also hunt during the day. Because Arctic winter days are short and summer days are exceptionally long, Arctic foxes hunt day or night.

When not hunting, foxes rest. Some species prefer to sleep in their dens. This is true of desert species that avoid the hot sun by sleeping in their cool, dark dens. Arctic species also sleep in dens when temperatures drop far below zero. Foxes in **temperate** climates sleep anywhere. They use dens for birthing and raising cubs, but will sleep under piles of logs or back porches or in barns.

Some fox species use one den for birthing and other dens for sleeping. A birthing den stinks. Foxes normally have a fairly unpleasant, musky odor, similar to that of skunks, that comes from a scent gland found at the base of the tail. In a birthing den, mother and kits combine their stench, creating quite a foul smell. Adults use this strong scent to mark the family's territory.

Most fox families are territorial. They mark the patch of land in which they live, hunt, and produce their young. Male and female foxes can reproduce when they are ten months old. Mating pairs usually produce litters of one to

thirteen pups. The litter size depends on the species and the amount of food available in the area. During one life span, an adult may produce several dozen young. If only half of those young survive and produce more young, the fox population thrives.

A mother red fox tends to her young in a den.

Did You Know?
For at least three weeks after giving birth, a vixen remains in the den, nursing her young. Her partner will hunt for her, providing the fox version of breakfast in bed.

Fox pups have short childhoods. The kits' eyes open when they are two weeks old. They grow rapidly as they nurse, fed on rich mother's milk and later on meat. At first, meat is pre-chewed by a parent because it is easier to digest that way. Within ten weeks, kits are completely weaned from nursing and they are learning to hunt on their own. By ten months old, kits are adults and can produce young. For some fox species, this is a time of **dispersal**—a period when a family's young move away to find their own territories and set up their own dens.

Foxes are clever critters. Why bother to dig a den when there are empty homes available? Swift foxes (*Vulpes velox*) often move into abandoned prairie dog dens. Cape foxes (*Vulpes chama*) in South Africa find that aardvarks leave behind several quality home sites.

Even with ready-made homes and plentiful food, foxes do not normally live very long. Rarely, foxes survive for up to twelve years, but most foxes usually die before they reach five or six years old. Foxes face a number of dangers. Wolves and coyotes are not just relatives, but also enemies. Smaller but equally deadly **predators** include eagles, wild dogs, bobcats, lynxes, and panthers. Foxes that live in Africa face hyenas, jackals, leopards, and lions. Foxes die of starvation, drowning, and disease. They are also trapped, shot, poisoned, and run over by humans.

Two young cheetahs chase after a bat-eared fox.

Chapter Four

Types of Foxes

A fennec fox (*Vulpes zerda*) pops its head out of its den. The fox's ears twitch. It can hear the footsteps of a cricket on the Sahara sands. The fennec's ears equal one-fifth of the animal's body surface. They allow the fennec to hear the movements of insects, lizards, and mice—the fox's favorite foods. The fennec's 10- to 15-centimeter (4- to 6-inch) ears perform another job—heat loss. Blood moves close to the surface of the ears and allows the body to shed excess heat.

Several species of foxes live in desert or semiarid regions. Fennec fox territories overlap the territories of Ruppell's foxes (*Vulpes rueppellii*) and pallid foxes (*Vulpes pallida*). All three species live in the Sahara, but the Ruppell's fox and the fennec fox can also be found on the Arabian Peninsula.

Blanford's foxes (*Vulpes cana*) live in mountain and desert areas of Afghanistan, Pakistan, Israel, Oman, and Iran. In North America, kit foxes find the dry deserts of the Southwest to their liking.

Did You Know?
Fennec foxes are the world's smallest foxes. Their bodies measure 24 to 40 centimeters (9.4 to 15.7 inches) long and weigh 0.8 to 1.5 kilograms (1.8 to 3.3 pounds).

How do foxes survive in such dry habitats? Desert foxes do drink from water holes, but they can get all the water they need from the food they eat. Their diet consists mostly of insects, lizards, eggs, and birds that nest, feed, and live on the ground. Those creatures have water in their bodies. Desert foxes tend to be among the smallest of fox species.

Because they live in the desert, Cape foxes, such as this one, get most of their water from the foods they eat.

While most fox species prefer to live alone, fennec, pallid, and Ruppell's foxes prefer close-knit communities. They share long, narrow dens, with several males, females, and young. Hunting is done alone because group hunting is not necessary for capturing a beetle or a mouse.

Did You Know?
While most fox species thrive on meat, Blanford's foxes eat mostly insects and small mammals but can survive by eating melons, grapes, and olives.

A fennec fox emerges from its den.

GRASSLANDS FOXES

A corsac fox (*Vulpes corsac*) leaps and pounces on a gerbil. Corsacs are nocturnal predators that catch plenty of gerbils, pikas, susliks, and jerboas. They also eat insects and birds when they can catch them. Corsacs are among the many fox species that thrive on grasslands. They live in Turkistan, Russia, Mongolia, Tibet, and Manchuria.

Grasslands provide a full range of prey for fox species. In Somalia, the bat-eared fox thrives on a diet of 80 percent insects. Bat-eared foxes specialize in eating harvester termites and dung beetles. In central Canada, swift foxes race across the Great Plains. They get their name from their ability to run 40 kilometers per hour (25 miles per hour). Like bat-eared foxes, swift foxes like to eat insects, especially grasshoppers. Swift foxes also hunt cottontails, jackrabbits, and kangaroo rats.

Most foxes that are found in grassland habitats form monogamous pairs. In some situations, both parents raise their young together. In other cases, the mothers work as single parents. While not "true" foxes, Crab-eating foxes (*Cerdocyon thous*) often live in family groups and can be seen feeding together. Corsac foxes live in large communities of connecting burrows that allow this social species to visit.

Corsacs may hunt together in small groups, depending on the prey available. Cape foxes, found on South African grasslands, live in pairs but hunt alone.

THE EVER-PRESENT RED FOX

Of all fox species, the most common is the red fox (*Vulpes vulpes*). Red foxes have the greatest worldwide distribution of any mammal except humans. They live along shorelines, in meadows and grasslands, and on mountains up to 4,500 meters (14,764 feet) high. Red foxes are survivors.

Corsac foxes can be found in grassy areas in Europe and Asia.

They can live in every environment, from hot deserts to Arctic tundra, rural farmland to urban parks.

Despite the name, not all red foxes have red fur. Some have white pelts. Others have silver or black coloring. They all have white chins and bellies and startling amber eyes that seem to glow in the dark.

The red fox is the species that appears in fables, fairy tales, and myths. They are widespread in Europe, Asia, North America, North Africa, and Australia. They live on the fringe of the Arctic tundra and in all temperate regions.

Red foxes are wily predators known for their speed. They can run up to about 77 kilometers per hour (48 miles per hour). Not fussy eaters, red foxes will ingest whatever food is present in their territories. Studies show that red foxes will eat nearly three dozen types of mammals, fourteen species of birds and their eggs, fifteen families of insects, and twenty-one types of plants. A hungry fox will eat worms, lizards, toads, and frogs. In cities, they pick through garbage and eat everything from leftover burgers to apple cores and candy bars. Nocturnal creatures, red foxes strike at twilight and at night. They are the ones that farmers usually blame when hens disappear from the henhouse or lambs disappear from the fields.

Did You Know?
Many foxes are raised on farms for their fur. Only minks are more common as farm-raised, furbearing mammals.

Dens appear regularly throughout the red fox's territory. A breeding pair may have one main den for birthing and several hidey-holes for making quick disappearances. Tunnels can measure 10 meters (32 feet) long, and the number of exits is limited only by the willingness of the foxes living there to dig.

Red foxes are common prey for golden eagles, wolves, coyotes, and bears. They also suffer from such diseases as distemper, rabies, and parvovirus, which also affect dogs. In the wild, foxes can suffer from ticks, **mange,** lice, fleas, tapeworms, heartworms, and hookworms. These conditions can also affect household pets. However, foxes are *not* pets. They do not adjust to living in homes. Even when taken in as young pups, foxes quickly change from cuddly pets to destructive, unmanageable pests.

A young red fox stands by the entrance to its den.

Chapter Five

The Past, Present, and Future

Foxes are part of the family Canidae, which also includes wolves, dogs, coyotes, and jackals. Early members of this family in North America evolved into foxes and wolves, the two major wild Canidae species on the continent today. The gray fox (*Urocyon cinereoargenteus*), found in southwestern United States and Central America, can trace its ancestors back six to nine million years. They are the oldest Canidae species in North America.

Between five and seven millions years ago, other ancient members of the family Canidae moved north toward the Bering land bridge. These animals traveled across the land bridge into Asia and moved on toward Europe. They spread across the continents, and these animals evolved into the twenty-three species of foxes that presently live worldwide. Of those species twelve are true or *Vulpes* foxes, and eleven belong to other genuses.

Half a million years ago, swift foxes made the return
journey from Asia to North America. Swift foxes moved
onto the Great Plains and settled in the vast grassy area.

Swift foxes, like the one shown here, live in the western United States.

They thrived until humans invaded the prairies and hunted them for their pelts.

THREATS TO SURVIVAL

Select species of foxes struggle to survive despite their ability to adapt to almost any environment. Foxes suffer from disease and predation, but their greatest problems come from humans.

Trapping foxes for their fur has reduced the fox populations in Canada, Alaska, northern Europe, and Russia. This is not a problem from times past. Foxes are still trapped for their fur in most U.S. states, Canada, Europe, and Asia. The fox-trapping industry peaked in the late 1970s, when the number of pelts traded ranged between 50,000 and 100,000 per year. Wearing furs may not be a popular fashion trend these days, but people still buy fox fur gloves, hats, scarves, earmuffs, and coats.

Foxhunting is considered an elegant sport by some and brutal inhumanity by others. British hunters meet protestors in the fields every time they mount their horses. Foxhunting is not new, but many British citizens would like to see the practice banned. Foxhunting accounts for less than one in ten deaths of wild foxes yearly.

Would You Believe?
About ten thousand years ago, gray foxes arrived on the northern Channel Islands off California. About three thousand years ago, a number of foxes migrated to the southern islands. Today, the northern and southern island foxes represent two different species—all endangered.

Hunting foxes in the general sense takes far more foxes from the wild each year than does organized fox-hunting with horses. Farmers believe that foxes hunt for food among their livestock. A chicken coop provides meat and eggs for a clever fox that can find a way in. Young

A pack of dogs leads the way during a foxhunting event in England.

lambs in open fields seem likely targets as well. Farmers with rifles and dogs make regular patrols of their land in search of foxes. What they fail to realize is that foxes actually help them. Foxes usually eat more rodents than livestock.

The worldwide population of Arctic foxes is neither threatened nor endangered. However, the small populations on Mednyi Island, Russia, and Fennoscandia (Norway, Sweden, Finland, and the Kola Peninsula) are in trouble. Mednyi Island has lost 85 to 90 percent of its Arctic foxes to mange. The Fennoscandia population has been low since the early twentieth century. The population was overhunted for fur and has never recovered.

FOXES IN THE NEWS

Recent events in Russia, Australia, and the Channel Islands of California have put foxes in the news. In Russia, forty-five years of careful breeding by researchers has produced tame foxes that are as much like pets as poodles are. The foxes have been selectively bred for placid personalities. Newborn fox pups in this experiment are as playful and gentle as dog puppies. This experiment is for professionals only—do not try this at home.

The news from Australia is worrisome. The island of Tasmania, off the southern coast of Australia, is an ecological wonder. It is home to extremely rare species, such as ground parrots, eastern quolls, and Tasmanian devils. Somehow, the red fox has arrived on the island. Finding the body of a red fox has caused Tasmanian officials to declare a national environmental emergency. Foxes are invasive species in Tasmania and put seventy-eight native species at risk of predation. Their arrival throws off the natural balance of nature on that unique island.

In the past fifteen years, the Channel Island fox populations on Santa Cruz, Santa Rosa, and San Miguel islands have gone from thriving to the brink of **extinction.** In the early 1990s, island fox populations went from about 1,500 animals per island to 14 on Santa Rosa, 15 on San Miguel, and fewer than 100 on Santa Cruz. Some foxes became the prey of golden eagles, which are also a protected species. Others died from a serious outbreak of canine distemper, a disease brought to the island by someone's pet dog. To protect the foxes from further distemper problems, cubs are found and vaccinated against the disease. The golden eagles are more difficult to deal with. They must be humanely captured and relocated.

REINTRODUCING SWIFT FOXES

One of **conservation**'s greatest success stories is the reintroduction of swift foxes to the Canadian Great Plains. During the twentieth century, the swift fox disappeared completely from the Canadian wild. Trapping for pelts was the biggest problem, although predation by red foxes and coyotes also reduced wild populations.

Several schoolchildren work with a veterinarian to release a fox into the wild in California.

With the help of conservationists, the swift fox is making a comeback.

In 1983, the Canadian Wildlife Service and several other agencies worked together to reintroduce the swift fox to the Canadian plains. Between 1983 and 1992, 643 foxes were released. Bad weather, coyotes, bobcats, eagles, and owls reduced the swift fox population, but some foxes survived. They produced young, and those young thrived. A census taken in 2000–2001 of the swift fox population in Alberta, Saskatchewan, and the state of Montana counted 877 animals. Ninety percent of those foxes were born in the wild.

Foxes perform a valuable service in the wild. They keep rodent populations under control and are part of nature's plan. Restoring a population such as that of the swift fox restores nature's balance on the prairie. Since humans caused the disappearance of foxes on the Great Plains, it is fitting that humans brought this species home again.

Glossary

cache (KASH) to collect and store food for later use

conservation (kon-sur-VAY-shun) the preservation or management of natural resources

dispersal (dis-PUR-sull) the act of moving away from the family unit, usually referring to animals in the wild

extinction (eks-TINK-shun) the state of a plant or animal no longer existing

gekker (GEK-kur) a short half-bark, half-cough noise made by foxes

genus (JEE-nuss) a group or class of related animals

mange (MAYNJ) a skin disease caused by parasitic mites, resulting in loss of hair, itchiness, and, in some animals, death

migrate (MY-grayt) to move from one place to another to live or find food

monogamous (muh-NOG-uh-muss) having one spouse or mating partner

nocturnal (nok-TUR-null) active at night

pallid (PAL-id) pale or light in color

permafrost (PUR-muh-frawst) continuously frozen subsoil

polynya (puh-LIN-yuh) a patch of unfrozen seawater surrounded by ice

predator (PREH-duh-tur) an animal that hunts and kills other animals for food

regurgitate (ree-GUR-juh-tayt) to vomit

temperate (TEM-per-ut) having weather that is not extremely hot or extremely cold

For More Information

Watch It

Alaska's Tundra Tails, VHS (Anchorage, AK: Alaska Video Postcards, Inc., 1996)

Really Wild Animals: Amazing North America, VHS (Washington, DC: National Geographic Video, 1997)

Wonders of Nature in Our Backyard: Birds, Frogs, Foxes, Dragonflies, and More!, DVD (Atlanta, GA: Marshall Fairman Productions, 2002)

Read It

Alexander, Bryan and Cherry. *Journey into the Arctic*. New York: Oxford University Press, 2003.

Hanson, Jonathan and Roseann. *Desert Dogs: Coyotes, Foxes, & Wolves*. Tuscon, AZ: Arizona-Sonora Desert Museum Press, 1996.

Henry, J. Daniel. *Red Fox*. Washington, DC: Smithsonian, 1996.

Levine, Michelle. *Red Foxes*. Minneapolis, MN: Lerner Publications, 2004.

Macdonald, David. *Foxes*. Stillwater, MN: Voyageur Press, 2000.

Somervill, Barbara A. *Tundra*. Chanhassen, MN: Traditions Publishing, 2004.

Tweit, Susan. *City Foxes*. Portland, OR: Alaska Northwest Books, 1997.

Look It Up

Visit our Web page for lots of links about foxes:
http://www.childsworld.com/links

Note to Parents, Teachers, and Librarians: We routinely verify our Web links to make sure they are safe, active sites—so encourage your readers to check them out!

The Animal Kingdom
Where Do Foxes Fit In?

Kingdom: Animalia

Phylum: Chordata (animals with backbones)

Class: Mammalia

Order: Carnivora

Family: Canidae

Genus: *Vulpes*

Index

About the Author

Sophie Lockwood is a former teacher and a longtime writer. She writes textbooks, newspaper articles, and magazine articles. Sophie enjoys writing about animals and their habits. The most interesting part of her research, Sophie says, is learning how scientists apply their knowledge to save endangered species. She lives with her husband in the foothills of the Blue Ridge Mountains.